21st
Century
Junior
Library

FARM ANIMALS
SHEEP

by Cecilia Minden

CHERRY LAKE PUBLISHING * ANN ARBOR, MICHIGAN

CHERRY LAKE
Publishing

Published in the United States of America by Cherry Lake Publishing
Ann Arbor, Michigan
www.cherrylakepublishing.com

Content Adviser: Laurie Rincker, Assistant Professor of Agriculture, Eastern Kentucky University

Photo Credits: Cover and page 4, ©iStockphoto.com/martb; cover and page 6, ©marilyn barbone, used under license from Shutterstock, Inc.; page 8, ©iStockphoto.com/josuar; cover and page 10, ©iStockphoto.com/tseybold; page 12, ©iStockphoto.com/Murdo; page 14, ©Denis Pepin, used under license from Shutterstock, Inc.; page 16, ©iStockphoto.com/suemack; cover and page 18, ©Gail Johnson, used under license from Shutterstock, Inc.; page 20, ©Kgtoh/Dreamstime.com

LIBRARY OF CONGRESS CATALOGING-IN-PUBLICATION DATA
Minden, Cecilia.
 Farm animals: Sheep / by Cecilia Minden.
   p. cm.—(21st century junior library)
 Includes index.
 ISBN-13: 978-1-60279-544-0
 ISBN-10: 1-60279-544-4
 1.Sheep—Juvenile literature. I. Title. II. Title: Sheep. III. Series.
 SF375.2.M567 2010
 636.3—dc22   2009003318

Cherry Lake Publishing would like to acknowledge the work of
The Partnership for 21st Century Skills.
Please visit www.21stcenturyskills.org for more information.

CONTENTS

Sheep are interested in the world around them.

Who Says Baa?

Did you learn the nursery rhyme "Mary Had a Little Lamb" when you were small? Do you remember the words? Are sheep really "as white as snow"? Would a sheep follow you everywhere? Is this true of all sheep? Let's see what we can learn about sheep.

Lambs drink milk from their mothers.

White As Snow

Most sheep are white. Some are black, brown, gray, silver, or red. An adult male sheep is a **ram**. An adult female is called a **ewe**. A ewe gives birth to a lamb. She sometimes has three lambs at one time. Sheep can live between 10 and 20 years.

Sheep know one another by smell.

Sheep have a sharp sense of smell. They use it to find food and water. They can also smell when a **predator** is near. Their hearing is very good. They will turn their ears in the direction of sounds. Sheep also have excellent eyesight. They can even see what is behind them without turning all the way around!

Sheep need a lot of space to graze.

Sheep like to eat plants in the fields. They **graze** about 7 hours a day. They like to eat early in the morning or late in the day. This is because the weather is cooler at these times. Healthy sheep can **adapt** to most climates.

Look!

Mutton busting is a rodeo event in Canada. Children from 4 to 7 years old can enter. Riders sit on the backs of sheep. They try to stay on a sheep for 6 seconds. Helmets are a must!

A llama helps keep a flock together.

Flock of Followers

Sheep are natural followers. Young lambs are trained by other sheep. A flock will follow a lead sheep even if it brings them harm. Sheep owners use trained dogs, llamas, or donkeys to herd and guard the sheep.

A hungry coyote will attack sheep for food.

Sheep have few ways to defend themselves. When faced with a predator, they will flee or band together in a tight group. A sheep left out of the group is open to attack.

Sheep have many natural predators. Coyotes account for the largest number of sheep deaths. **Domestic** dogs are next. Bobcats and foxes also attack sheep.

Pet lambs depend on their owners to take care of them.

Many people like having sheep for pets. Do you think you would like a pet sheep? It would need clean food and water every day. It would also need to have its **fleece sheared**. Professional shearers can do this very quickly!

Think!

Lambs are usually not afraid of humans. They will let you feed them milk from bottles. The more you feed the lamb, the more it will trust you. Why do you think this is?
Hint: Who usually feeds a new lamb?

Sheep are not hurt when farmers
clip off their fleece.

Shop a Sheep

Sheep provide us with many products. Many sheep are raised for their wool. Wool comes from the sheep's fleece. Wool is in high demand for clothing. Wool is also used to make chairs, rugs, and even tennis balls!

Many people enjoy lamb meat as part
of a healthy dinner.

Sheep are also raised for meat, milk, and cheese.

Now you know that Mary's lamb can do much more than follow her to school!

Ask Questions!

Sheepherders in Ireland brand their sheep with special paint. Do some library research. See if you can learn why they paint their sheep. Asking questions is a good way to learn new information.

GLOSSARY

adapt (uh-DAPT) to change and fit in better

domestic (duh-MES-tik) bred by humans to not be wild

ewe (YOO) an adult female sheep

fleece (FLEES) wool taken from an animal at shearing

graze (GRAYZ) to feed on grass in the field

mutton (MUHT-un) meat from a sheep

predator (PRED-uh-tur) animal that hunts other animals for food

ram (RAM) an adult male sheep

sheared (SHEERD) to cut off hair or fleece

FIND OUT MORE

BOOKS

Murray, Julie. *Sheep*. Edina, MN: ABDO Publishing Company, 2005.

Nelson, Robin. *Sheep*. Minneapolis: Lerner Publications, 2009.

WEB SITES

Shearing World—Sheep Information for Children
www.shearingworld.com/ sheep_for%20children.htm
Photos and facts about sheep

Sheep 101
www.sheep101.info/index.html
Basic, fun information about different kinds of sheep and sheep products

INDEX

ABOUT THE AUTHOR

Cecilia Minden, PhD, is a literacy consultant and author of many books for children. She lives with her family near Chapel Hill, North Carolina. Cecilia and her husband, Dave, saw many painted sheep on their trip to Ireland.